Gifts from the Muse

Poetry from the Edge

By Kathryn Streletzky

Hovering...1

Sangria...3

Constellation 3

Candy..5

Vortex 7

Edge..9

YVHV..11

Mirror..11

SHE...13

Whispers...15

Priestess...17

Vapor...19

Wonder 21

Hovering

*The first three lines of this poem came on me
as in a fever. I had been visiting San Francisco
at the same time as my Muse, but at different
events. On the way home, the rest of the poem
came to me and I pulled across three lanes of
traffic so that I could write it down.*

Ever am I drawn to you,
A Moth to the Flame
Hovering. . . .

Like the photographer
In Marilyn's last sitting,
Longing with desire and champagne and
Three days of sweat

Wanting, not daring,
Seeking the immortality of passion
Captured in black and white

The famous close-up,
Taken from a ladder

So we hover,
And for an instant –
Are melded with Eternity

A Wave
About to break
Poised in transcendence
Before crashing into foam

Sangria

On returning from a business trip, I discovered
my Muse and his girlfriend strewn across my
bed-sheets bathed in moonlight. Next day, she
made us pancakes, while I made Sangria.

Constellation

I originally called this one Stars, but changed
the title to emphasis the inherent connection
among all things.

I drink you up
Not as a fine wine
But as Sangria
Full of gusto and glee
Our flavors
Mingling
Tingling
Delighting

Satisfying
As a catnap on the beach
Snuggling into a perfect fit
Happy with the day as we find it

Connect the dots
        That's all . . .
The Stars themselves
        Align in Constellation

Candy

Sweet, sweet memories welling up from another time, another place.

Getting of the plane
   In Hispaniola,
I just want to fuck

The night breeze clobbers me,
With its sweet-sweaty blast of humidity
   the scent of overripe fruit bathed in salt air

Mirrored ceilings – stained sheets
The tawdry morphs fresh and wonderful
     Like the slightly sour cheese we buy,
Lushness abounding in taste
     Salt on skin
Lime crisping on the fish, freshly fried

The ocean thrusts in sensual rhythms
And I respond in kind –
Melting all over him, like candy

Vortex

On a fine day in May, the ocean just stopped
and became as still as a lake for several days.
I always found this freakish when it happened

The stillness of the ocean
    Creates a vortex
Not unlike the VOID
    Mother of 10,000 things

And here I am
    Rebel newly created
This one with a cause
    Fanning a fire of lust

And the vortex, ancient mother,
    Brings me my desire
Just as I asked for it – no more, no less

Speak and it shall be given unto you

A precious gift
Sap rising again with the Spring
Flowing into Maple Sugar

Edge

Inspired by Carlos Castaneda and Joseph Chilton Pearce, this poem became part of my memoir. RiverRun: Adventures on the Edge of Enlightenment.

The Edge of Enlightenment
       is not calculus
There's no approaching zero

There's only dancing on the
       Edge itself
And throwing it all away

Perspective shifts,
And all that is, Is –
Laser light shining through
The Crack in the Cosmic Egg

YVHV

*Recognizing the god/goddess within with a tip
of the hat to Joseph Campbell's **Thou Art That**.*

Mirror

*I was missing my Muse when I wrote this: that
darn ocean turning still stirred me up again.*

I feel like myself
        Again

And wonder who
        I am as
Apart from myself

I am
That

Thou art
That

I AM

The stillness of the ocean
        Mirrors my heart
Neither reaching out
        Nor receding

Exploring all the empty places
        Water runs deep
And silent

SHE

I call this one SHE because I had taken a Monroe Institute workshop group up on Mount Shasta. When Robert Monroe first developed his acoustic technology for out of body exploration, a woman he identified as SHE became one of his Explorers in these altered states of consciousness. Seemed fitting for the SHE we encountered on the mountain that afternoon.

Sought on the Mountain
No seeker SHE
Treading down steep & rocky
Unshod
Elegantly draped in muslin
Baby Butterfly on hip
No, not the winged creature –
A beautiful tow headed blue eyed boy

Her own baby blues twinkle at my questions
Her lips shimmer as with glitter
And SHE answers with notes from a flute
Held in her hand, the one without Butterfly

First there was a mountain
        Then there was no mountain
            Then there was

How old is SHE?
Looking all of 15
And 15 thousand years
Timeless in beauty, grace
Wisdom

Seekers, we
Struggling up
Each step
We encounter SHE
And find the magic in ourselves
SHE is the me we are seeking

Whispers

I said goodbye to my beautiful sister when she was just 35. As she lost her physical capacity, she rarely lamented her restrictions. She chose to live at home for her final months, and took up bird-watching. I wanted to honor her as the Tibetan monks do, casting the last remnants of her body to the vultures. Linda is still here as the best part of me.

She only whispers of death
Whispers so softly that
        no words are spoken

No words are needed
        I hear her whispers

And I want to shout
        "Let me toss your limbs
        to the buzzards"

You're dying!
And the secrets
of the world are revealed
by a bluebird near the window

You're dying!
And so our own
returns to the clouds
Ocean no more

I'll look for you in the sky

Priestess

While I was celebrating my birthday in Mount Shasta, Joseph Campbell style, by hosting a workshop, I treated myself to a couple of bronze sculptures by Mary Saint-Marie. Plus, I was reading a lot about the rocket scientist Jack Parsons that summer too. My Muse thinks this is my best piece, and I agree.

Lillith
Isis
Babylon Whore

Serpent Priestess
Am I –
Manifesting
the pleasures of 10,000 things

From the rib of Adam say they –
One brings forth Two

Two brings forth Three
And then the whole of creation
From the Mother Womb

We choose Experience
Casting ourselves out of the Garden

Striving to Remember
Who we really are –
Gods and Goddesses in human form

Seekers of Bliss
Eternal
Transcending

The Universe
Alive
Conscious
Evolving

Vapor

Now my Muse hated this poem because he believes in the Self and Self-ish-ness. I don't think he recognized the opening lines as being from a Joseph Campbell lecture. And it's ironic too, because I wrote this about the time when he moved into my home, and I started taking care of him in little ways, like cooking for him.

No self – No problem
    Said the Wise Monk

And so I will retreat from this world
    Never meant for me
10,000 things – signifying nothing

Many faces of Moon
    Constant through its changes
Always, All ways
    Mirroring Central Sun

Love without Conditions
    The Brilliance of Hyperion
Reflected back through every mood

Yang flames forth
    In Darkness
Welcomed by the Void

Quenched by the Fire
    The Waters of Yin
Return to Source
    As Vapor

Wonder

A great love that's eternal, and yet . . . lost. I miss my Muse, though he is with me, always

Everything changes
Memory shifts its view

I long not for passionate kisses
Only for the way
        Your lips
Guppied up to greet me
        After a long absence

Everything changes
True love says Fare Well

On mornings like these,
I'd walk along the ocean
        while you slept

Happy returning home
Knowing you were there
        Eventually spouting up
                Like the whales do
Singing your song of wonder
        As if it were for me

Made in the USA
Monee, IL
25 June 2023

37307972R00015